Key Stage 1 Maths Practice Test Papers

Author: Brad Thompson

Contents

Instructions

Introduction

This practice resource consists of three complete sets of Key Stage 1 maths practice test papers. Each set contains test papers similar to those that pupils will take at the end of Year 2. They can be used at any time throughout the year to provide practice for the Key Stage 1 tests.

The result of the papers will provide a good idea of pupils' strengths and weaknesses.

Administering the Tests

- Children should work in a quiet environment where they can complete each test undisturbed and you can give the prompts required.

- Children should have a pen or pencil, ruler, eraser and protractor. A calculator is not allowed.

- Handwriting is not assessed but children should write their answers clearly.

- Explain that the first question on each paper is a practice question. Before proceeding to question 1, ensure that children know where they should have written their answer and discuss with them how they worked out their answer.

- Children should try to answer all of the questions. If they can't answer a question, they should move on to the next one and come back to that one later. Remind them that you can't help answer the questions and that they need to work them out on their own.

- The amount of time per test varies. The Key Stage 1 tests are not strictly timed and it is up to you to decide when or if a break is required during these practice tests. Below is a guide to approximately how long each test is expected to take:
  - **Paper 1 arithmetic** – 20 minutes
  - **Paper 2 reasoning** – 35 minutes

Aural Questions Administration (Paper 2)

The instructions below are for the first five questions in each Paper 2 (the reasoning papers). After the practice question, questions 1 to 5 are aural questions.

Read questions 1 to 5 out loud, allowing time at the end of each question for children to write their answers.

For **Set A Paper 2:**
Read out these questions. Children should listen carefully and write their answers on pages 31–33.

P. Eve has 10 buttons. Tick the largest button.

1. Max has four friends: James, Anisa, Sanjay and Fatima. He gives ten pence to each friend. How much money does he give altogether? Write your answer in the box.

2. Look at the triangle. Part of the triangle is shaded. Tick the fraction that is equal to the shaded part of the triangle. Put your tick in the box next to the correct fraction.

3. Look at the array of circles. Now look at the four calculations. Tick the calculation that describes the array of circles.

4. Tick the number that is 150.

5. Write down all the even numbers between fifteen and twenty-five.

For **Set B Paper 2:**

Read out these questions. Children should listen carefully and write their answers on pages 59–61.

P. Look at the bag. How many marbles are inside the bag? Write your answer in the box.

1. I am counting backwards. When I stop counting, write the next two numbers I should say: 93, 92, 91, 90... Write your answers in the boxes.

2. What is thirty take away five, take away another five? Write your answer in the box.

3. There are 18 buttons in a box. The box can hold twenty-five buttons. How many more buttons can fit in the box? Write your answer in the box.

4. Write the same number in both boxes to make the multiplication correct.

5. Two of the shapes are hexagons. Tick the two hexagons.

For **Set C Paper 2:**

Read out these questions. Children should listen carefully and write their answers on pages 87–89.

P. Look at the four ladders. Tick the tallest ladder.

1. Sort the glasses from most full to least full. Write the letters in the boxes in the correct order. One is done for you.

2. Look at the boat. The boat sails to one of the islands. It sails three squares forward. The boat then turns a quarter of a turn clockwise and sails forward four squares. Circle the island the boat sails to.

3. There are eighty-five tennis balls in a large tub. Max takes ten tennis balls away. How many tennis balls are left in the large tub? Write your answer in the box.

4. An orange costs 20p. How much do two oranges cost? Write your answer in the box.

5. Three of the shapes are regular polygons. Tick the three regular polygons.

Marking the Tests

Each set of maths practice papers is worth a total of 60 marks:

- Paper 1 arithmetic is worth 25 marks.⎤
- Paper 2 reasoning is worth 35 marks.⎦   Total = 60 marks

Use the answers section to mark the test papers. Add up the total marks for Paper 1 and Paper 2. As a general guideline, if a child gets 36 or more marks across the two papers (i.e. 36 or more out of 60), they are reaching the expected standard.

Keep in mind that the exact number of marks required to achieve the expected standard may vary year by year depending on the overall difficulty of the test.

Answers

Content domain coverage for the questions in this paper is shown in the tables of answers below. Information about these codes can be found in the KS1 Maths test framework.

Set A Paper 1: Arithmetic

Question (Content domain)		Requirement	Mark	Additional guidance
P		6	none	Practice question
1	1C2a	9	1	
2	1C2a	20	1	
3	2C6	50	1	
4	1F1a	4	1	
5	2C2b	46	1	
6	2C1	70	1	
7	2N1/2C2b	48	1	
8	2C2a	30	1	
9	2N1/2C1	80	1	
10	2C2b	79	1	
11	2C2b	69	1	
12	2C6	18	1	
13	2C2b	99	1	
14	2C6	5	1	
15	1C4	7	1	
16	2C2b	72	1	
17	2C2b	100	1	
18	2C2b	39	1	
19	2N1/2N6	104	1	
20	2N6/2C2b	67	1	
21	2C2b	45	1	
22	2C2b	95	1	
23	2C6	12	1	
24	2C3	70	1	
25	2F1a	5	1	

Set A Paper 2: Reasoning

Question (Content domain)		Requirement	Mark	Additional guidance
P		Largest button ticked as shown: ✓	none	Practice question Accept any other clear way of indicating the correct answer.
1	2C8	40 (p)	1	
2	2F1a/2F2	The correct fraction ticked as shown: $\frac{1}{2}$ ✓	1	Accept any other clear way of indicating the correct answer. Do not award the mark if additional fractions are indicated, unless it is clear the correct fraction is the pupil's final choice.
3	2C8	The correct calculation ticked as shown: 3 x 4 ✓	1	Accept any other clear way of indicating the correct answer. Do not award the mark if additional calculations are indicated, unless it is clear the correct calculation is the pupil's final choice.
4	2N2a	150 ticked	1	Accept any other clear way of indicating the correct answer. Do not award the mark if additional numbers are indicated, unless it is clear the correct number is the pupil's final choice.
5	2C6/2N2a/2N3	16, 18, 20, 22, 24	1	All five numbers must be written down for the award of the mark. The numbers can be written in any order.
6	1M1	Letters in correct order as shown: D, C, B, A	1	All letters must be in the correct order for the award of the mark. Accept any other clear way of indicating the correct answer, e.g. matching each car to its correct position.
7	2N2b	Numbers in correct order as shown: 56, 60, 65, 69, 96	1	All numbers must be in the correct order for the award of the mark. Accept any other clear way of indicating the correct answer, e.g. matching each number to its correct position. Accept the numbers given in the reverse order, provided the labels have been swapped.
8	2N6/2C3	28	1	
9	1P2	Just below the third black section ticked as shown: ✓	1	Accept any other clear way of indicating the correct answer. Do not award the mark if more than one section has been indicated, unless it is clear that just below the third black section is the pupil's final choice.

Question (Content domain)		Requirement	Mark	Additional guidance
10	2C6	Both correct numbers circled as shown: (15,) 56, (39,) 90	1	Both numbers must be indicated for the award of the mark. Accept any other clear way of indicating the two correct numbers. Do not award the mark if additional numbers are indicated, unless it is clear that the two correct numbers are the pupil's final choice.
11	2C1	35 (sweets)	1	
12	2C4	69(cm)	1	
13	2M2	10(cm)	1	Accept 100mm
14a	2S1	2 (bicycles)	1	
14b	2S2b	6 (cars)	1	
15	2C7/2C8	8 × 5 = 40 OR 5 × 8 = 40	1	All three numbers must be correct for the award of the mark.
16	2C1/2C3	Both numbers correct as shown: 12 9	1	Both numbers must be correct for the award of the mark.
17	2C9a	All number sentences completed as shown: 17 + 27 = 44 27 + 17 = 44 44 − 27 = 17 44 − 17 = 27	1	All numbers in all number sentences must be correct for the award of the mark.
18	2C8/2M3b	10 (coins)	1	
19	2C4	Award **TWO** marks for the three calculations completed correctly using six different numbers, e.g. 35 + 0, 34 + 1 and 33 + 2	Up to 2	**All three** calculations must be correct for the award of **TWO** marks. **Any two calculations** can be correct for the award of **ONE** mark. Award **ONE** mark if three calculations are correct but numbers are repeated in two of the calculations **or** there is an error in one of the calculations, e.g. 35 + 0, 0 + 35 and 34 + 1 OR 35 + 0, 34 + 1 and 33 + 3.
20	2G2a	Three shapes ticked as shown:	1	All three shapes must be indicated for the award of the mark. Accept any other clear way of indicating the three correct shapes. Do not award the mark if additional shapes are indicated, unless it is clear that the three correct shapes are the pupil's final choice.

Question (Content domain)		Requirement	Mark	Additional guidance
21	2M4c	24 (trains)	1	
22	2C8	16 (marbles)	1	
23	2N4	Correct number given as shown: ☐ 32 (number line)	1	
24	2C8/2M9	Award **TWO** marks for the correct answer of 80(p). If the answer is incorrect or missing, award **ONE** mark for evidence of a complete, correct method, e.g. • 25 + 25 + 10 + 10 + 10 = (incorrect or no answer) • 25 × 2 = 60 (error) 60 + 30 =	Up to 2	Use the example responses given to help determine how many marks can be awarded.
25	2F1a	Correct shape ticked as shown:	1	Accept any other clear way of indicating the correct shape. Do not award the mark if additional shapes are indicated, unless it is clear that the correct shape is the pupil's final choice.
26	2P2	2	1	
27	2M2/2C4	15(ml)	1	
28	2C4	Correct number sentence given: 5 × 6 = 30 OR 6 × 5 = 30 Accept other multiplication sentences with the product 30, except 1 × 30, e.g. 2 × 15 = 30 3 × 10 = 30	1	Award the mark even if additional correct or relevant calculations are given along with a correct calculation, e.g. • 3 × 5 = 15, 2 × 15 = 30 Also accept: 6 × 5 = 1 × 30 5 + 5 + 5 + 5 + 5 + 5 = 1 × 30 Do not accept 1 × 30 or 30 × 1 unless accompanied by an additional correct number sentence. Do not accept an incomplete number sentence e.g. 5 × 6 5 × 6 24 (missing equals sign) 5 × 6 = (missing product)
29	2C6/2C7/2C9b	60 ÷ 5 = 12 Accept 60 = 5 × 12	1	The correct symbol must be written in both boxes for the award of the mark.
30	2C8/2C4	Award **TWO** marks for the correct answer of 50 (grapes). If the answer is incorrect or missing, award **ONE** mark for evidence of a complete, correct method, e.g. • 8 × 10 – 30 = (incorrect or no answer) • 8 × 10 = 90 (error) 90 – 30 =	Up to 2	Use the example responses given to help determine how many marks can be awarded.
31	2C4	43 (grams)	1	

Set B Paper 1: Arithmetic

Question (Content domain)		Requirement	Mark	Additional guidance
P		8	none	Practice question
1	1C2a	3	1	
2	1C2a	14	1	
3	2C2b	49	1	
4	1N1b/2C1	30	1	
5	2C2b	70	1	
6	2C6	70	1	
7	2N1/2N6	10	1	
8	1F1a	5	1	
9	2C3/2C9a	26	1	
10	2C2b	78	1	
11	2C6	4	1	
12	2C2b	87	1	
13	2C2b	95	1	
14	2C6	20	1	
15	2C1/2N6	50	1	
16	2C2b	91	1	
17	2C6	0	1	
18	2C2b	24	1	
19	2C2b	100	1	
20	2C2b	37	1	
21	2C6	9	1	
22	2C3/2C9a	65	1	
23	2F1a	8	1	
24	2C3	10	1	
25	2C2b	72	1	

Set B Paper 2: Reasoning

Question (Content domain)		Requirement	Mark	Additional guidance
P		5 (marbles)	none	Practice question
1	1N1a	89, 88	1	
2	2N1	20	1	
3	2C4	7 (buttons)	1	
4	2C6/2C8	10 × 10	1	
5	2G1a/2G2a	The two hexagons ticked as shown: 	1	Both correct shapes must be indicated for the award of the mark. Accept any other clear way of indicating the two correct shapes. Do not award the mark if additional shapes are indicated, unless it is clear that the two correct shapes are the pupil's final choice.
6	2N6	Smallest 169 Largest 961	1	Both correct numbers must be written for the award of the mark.
7	1G1a	All three shapes ticked as shown: triangle ✓ square ✓ rectangle circle ✓ hexagon	1	Three correct shapes must be indicated for the award of the mark. Accept any other clear way of indicating the three correct shapes. Do not award the mark if additional shapes are indicated, unless it is clear that the three correct shapes are the pupil's final choice.
8	2M4b/2M4c	Longest time circled: 65 minutes	1	Accept any other clear way of indicating the correct answer. Do not award the mark if additional times are indicated, unless it is clear that the correct time is the pupil's final choice.
9	2P1	Star ticked as shown: 	1	Accept any other clear way of indicating the correct shape. Do not award the mark if additional shapes are indicated, unless it is clear that the correct shape is the pupil's final choice.
10	2C6	45 (pencils)	1	
11	2M9	25(p)	1	
12	2C2b	47 (satsumas)	1	
13	1N4	57	1	

Question (Content domain)		Requirement	Mark	Additional guidance
14	2N2b	Both inequalities completed correctly, using each of the given numbers once only, e.g. 3 < 27 and 40 < 76 OR 3 < 40 and 27 < 76 OR 3 < 76 and 27 < 40	1	Both inequalities must be correct for the award of the mark. Do not award the mark if any number is used more than once, e.g. 3 < 27 27 < 76 Do not award the mark if numbers not given in the question are used.
15	2C1/2C2a/2C3	52 − 25 = 27	1	Both correct numbers must be written for the award of the mark.
16	2C8	6 (ice cubes)	1	Also accept the word 'six' written as long as it is clear it is the pupil's final answer.
17	2M3a/2M9	85(p)	1	Do not award the mark if the correct coins are indicated but their total value of 85p is not given, e.g. 50p, 20p, 10p and 5p circled without a total.
18	2N4	Correct numbers given as shown:	1	The correct numbers must be written in the boxes for the award of the mark.
19	2C9b	Both number sentences completed as shown: 12 × 10 = 120 120 ÷ 12 = 10 OR 12 × 10 = 120 120 ÷ 10 = 12	1	All numbers in both number sentences must be correct for the award of the mark.
20	2C4/2C2b	92 (buses)	1	
21	2C6/2C8	Calculations circled as shown: 10 + 4 (4 × 10) (10 + 10 + 10 + 10) 4 + 4 + 4 + 4	1	Accept any other clear way of indicating the correct answer. Do not award the mark if additional calculations are indicated, unless it is clear that the correct calculations are the pupil's final choice.

Question (Content domain)	Requirement	Mark	Additional guidance
22 2C1/2C2b	Award **TWO** marks for two number sentences completed correctly, using four different number cards from those that are given, e.g. 10 + 70 30 + 50 45 + 35 Award **ONE** mark for one number sentence completed correctly using the given cards, e.g. 45 + 35 Award **ONE** mark if the number sentences are correct, but the pupil has used the same number cards for both number sentences, e.g. 30 + 50 50 + 30	Up to 2	Accept any other clear way of indicating the correct answers, e.g. matching correct cards to answer boxes. Do not award any marks if the pupil uses numbers that are not given in the question.
23 1G1b	Cuboids ticked as shown: 	1	Accept any other clear way of indicating the correct shapes. Do not award the mark if additional shapes are indicated, unless it is clear that the correct shapes are the pupil's final choice.
24 2M2	50(ml)	1	
25a 2S2b	3 (children)	1	
25b 2S1	One block added to the cat column as shown: 	1	Accept inaccuracies in drawing the block as long as the intention is clear, e.g. a mark of any height between 5 and 6 on the vertical axis.
26 2C1/2C3	Number sentences completed correctly as shown: 44 + 6 = 50 94 + 6 = 100	1	Both number sentences must be completed correctly for the award of the mark.

Question (Content domain)		Requirement	Mark	Additional guidance
27	2C1/2M3a	Toys ticked as shown: 	1	Accept any other clear way of indicating the correct toys. Do not award the mark if additional toys are indicated, unless it is clear that the correct toys are the pupil's final choice.
28	2C4	15 written in both boxes	1	The correct number must be written in both boxes for the award of the mark.
29	2C4	Award **TWO** marks for the correct answer of 20 (cakes). If the answer is incorrect or missing, award **ONE** mark for evidence of a complete, correct method, e.g. 75 − 30 − 25 = (incorrect or no answer) 25 + 30 = 45 (error) 75 − 55 =	Up to 2	Use the example responses given to help determine how many marks can be awarded.
30	2F1a	Correct shape ticked as shown: 	1	Accept any other clear way of indicating the correct shape. Do not award the mark if additional shapes are indicated, unless it is clear that the correct shape is the pupil's final choice.
31	2C4	Number sentence completed as shown: 16 − 6 = 10 + 0	1	
32	2P2	3	1	Also accept the word 'three' written as long as it is clear it is the pupil's final answer.

Set C Paper 1: Arithmetic

Question (Content domain)		Requirement	Mark	Additional guidance
P		2	none	Practice question
1	1C1/1C2a	10	1	
2	1C1	0	1	
3	2C1	100	1	
4	1F1a	6	1	
5	2C1/2C2b	99	1	
6	2C2b/2N6	110	1	
7	2C6	9	1	
8	2C1	70	1	
9	2C6	80	1	
10	2C2b	97	1	
11	2N1/2C2b	14	1	
12	2C6	18	1	
13	2C2b	98	1	
14	2F1a	12	1	
15	2C3	50	1	
16	2C2b	64	1	
17	2C2b	97	1	
18	2C6	55	1	
19	2C2b	32	1	
20	1C1/2C1	15	1	
21	2C2b	25	1	
22	2C2b	9	1	
23	2F1a	6	1	
24	2C3/2C9a	68	1	
25	2C2b	83	1	

Question (Content domain)	Requirement	Mark	Additional guidance
P	Tallest ladder ticked as shown:	none	Practice question
1 IMI	Letters put in correct order as shown: D, A, C, B	1	All letters must be in the correct order for the award of the mark. Accept any other clear way of indicating the correct answer, e.g. matching each glass to its correct position.
2 2P2	Correct island circled as shown:	1	
3 2N6/2C2b	75 (tennis balls)	1	
4 2C1	40(p)	1	
5 2G1a/2G2a	Three regular polygons ticked as shown:	1	Three correct shapes must be indicated for the award of the mark. Accept any other clear way of indicating the three correct shapes. Do not award the mark if additional shapes are indicated, unless it is clear that the three correct shapes are the pupil's final choice.
6 2N1	Both numbers written in the boxes as shown: 0 **3** 6 9 **12**	1	Both numbers must be correct for the award of the mark.
7 2N3	68	1	Accept sixty-eight or sixty eight (including incorrect spelling that is plausibly 'sixty-eight')
8 2F1a	Any two-quarters shaded as shown:	1	Accept any other clear way of indicating two-quarters, e.g. marking the appropriate number of sections. Accept slight inaccuracies in shading. Do not award the mark if more or less than two-quarters has been shaded and the intention is not clear.
9 2C4/2M9	(£)7	1	Accept any unambiguous indication of the correct amount, e.g. (£)7.00 (£)7.00p 700p

Question (Content domain)		Requirement	Mark	Additional guidance
10	2F2	Correct answer circled as shown: $\frac{1}{3}$ $\frac{1}{2}$ ⊘$\frac{1}{4}$ $\frac{2}{4}$	1	Accept any other clear way of indicating the correct answer. Do not award the mark if more than one fraction has been indicated, unless it is clear that the correct fraction is the pupil's final choice.
11	2M4b/2M4c	Longest time ticked as shown: Journey to School (35 minutes) · Journey to Swimming (half an hour) · Journey to the Seaside (65 minutes) · Journey to Drama Club (2 hours) ✓	1	Accept any other clear way of indicating the correct answer. Do not award the mark if more than one journey has been indicated, unless it is clear that the correct journey is the pupil's final choice.
12	2M4a	The correct time ticked as shown: 1 o'clock · half past 1 · quarter to 1 · quarter past 1 ✓	1	Accept any other clear way of indicating the correct answer. Do not award the mark if additional times are indicated, unless it is clear that the correct time is the pupil's final choice.
13	2C8	12 (weeks)	1	
14	2S1/2S2b	7 (buttons)	1	
15	2C8	10 (pencils)	1	
16	2C4	(£)81	1	
17	2G2a	Three shapes ticked as shown: (cup) ✓ (key) ✓ (chair) ✓	1	Accept any other clear way of indicating the correct shapes. Do not award the mark if more or fewer than three shapes have been indicated, unless it is clear that the correct shapes are the pupil's final choice.
18	2F2	Correct fraction circled as shown: $\frac{1}{3}$ $\frac{1}{4}$ ⊘$\frac{2}{4}$ $\frac{2}{3}$	1	Accept any other clear way of indicating the correct fraction. Do not award the mark if additional fractions are indicated, unless it is clear the correct fraction is the pupil's final choice. Do not accept alternative equivalent values written, e.g. the word 'half'.
19	2C6/2C8	40 (children)	1	
20	2C4	Award **TWO** marks for the correct answer of 36 (people). If the answer is incorrect or missing, award **ONE** mark for evidence of a complete, correct method, e.g. • 62 + 19 − 45 = (incorrect or no answer) • 62 + 19 = 80 (error) 80 − 45 = 35	Up to 2	Use the example responses given to help determine how many marks can be awarded.
21	2N4	Correct numbers given as shown: 40 45 50 (number line from 35 to 55)	1	All three numbers must be correct for the award of the mark.
22	2C8/2C9b	9 (friends)	1	

Question (Content domain)	Requirement	Mark	Additional guidance
23 2M9/2M3a	Award the mark for a correct combination of coins ticked that totals 55p, i.e. • 50p and 5p • 20p, 10p, 10p, 10p and 5p	1	Accept any other clear way of indicating a correct combination of coins. Do not award the mark if additional coin combinations are indicated, unless it is clear the correct coin combination is the pupil's final choice.
24 2C3/2C2b	Calculation completed correctly as shown: $12 - 8 = 2 + 2$	1	
25 2C2b/2C1	Award **TWO** marks for the correct answer of 6 (spots). If the answer is incorrect or missing, award **ONE** mark for evidence of a complete, correct method, e.g. • $5 + 6 + 4 =$ (incorrect or no answer) • $5 + 6 + 4 = 15$ $21 - 15 = 5$ (error)	Up to 2	Use the example responses given to help determine how many marks can be awarded.
26 2N1	18	1	
27 1F1b	Square divided into four equal parts, e.g. 	1	Accept slight inaccuracies in drawing lines provided the intention is clear. Accept divisions that do not use dotted lines, provided the lines drawn are reasonably accurate, and the pupil's intention is clear, e.g. Do not award the mark if the square is divided into four unequal parts.
28 2M2	130(cm)	1	
29 2M2/1G1a	Rectangle drawn with the correct dimensions of 8cm x 4cm.	1	Accept any orientation of the rectangle. Accept slight inaccuracies of drawing as long as the intention is clear, allowing a tolerance of up to 5mm.
30 2G2b	Three correct shapes ticked as shown: 	1	Accept any other clear way of indicating the correct shapes. Do not award the mark if additional shapes are indicated, unless it is clear that the correct three shapes are the pupil's final choice.
31 2N2b/2N3/2C2a	Award **ONE** mark for any one of the following: $39 - 34$ $38 - 33$ $37 - 32$ $36 - 31$	1	
32a 1P2	Accept only B,4 OR B4	1	
32b 1P2	Accept any mark made in D3	1	

Key Stage 1

Set A

Mathematics

Paper 1: arithmetic

First Name	
Last Name	

Practice question

$$7 - 1 = \boxed{}$$

1

$5 + 4 =$ _____

1 mark

2

$29 - 9 =$ _____

1 mark

3

$5 \times 10 =$ _____

1 mark

4

$\dfrac{1}{2}$ of 8 =

1 mark

5

37 + 9 =

1 mark

6

20 + 50 =

1 mark

7

4 + 4 + 40 = ⬚

1 mark

8

35 − 5 = ⬚

1 mark

9

100 − 20 = ⬚

1 mark

10

5 + 74 = ☐

1 mark

11

56 + 13 = ☐

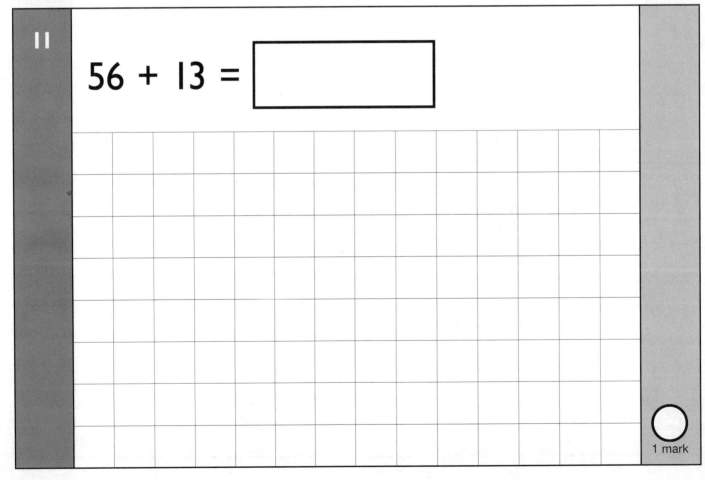

1 mark

12

$9 \times 2 = \boxed{}$

13

$66 + 33 = \boxed{}$

14

$10 \div 2 = \boxed{}$

15

$\boxed{} + 13 = 20$

16

87 – 15 = [ ]

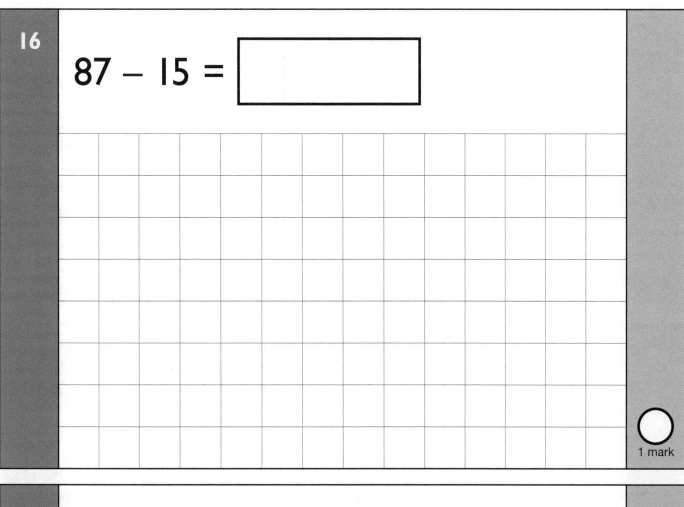

1 mark

17

55 + 45 = [ ]

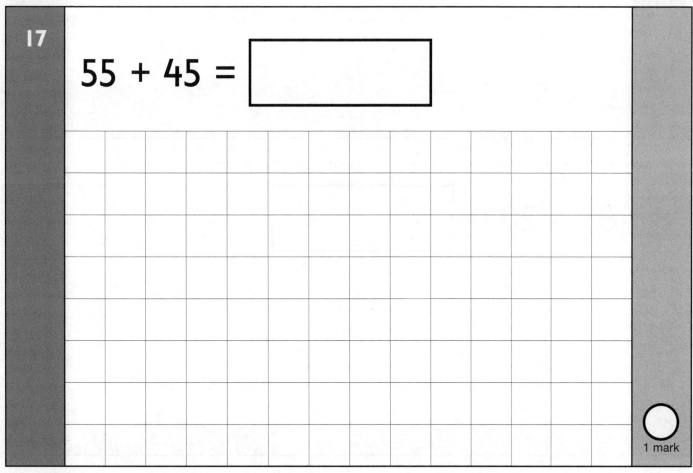

1 mark

18

$$44 - 5 = \boxed{}$$

◯
1 mark

19

$$94 + 10 = \boxed{}$$

◯
1 mark

20

$$87 - 20 = \boxed{}$$

◯
1 mark

21

$61 - 16 = \boxed{}$

1 mark

22

$26 + 69 = \boxed{}$

1 mark

23

$$60 \div 5 = \boxed{}$$

1 mark

24

$$77 - \boxed{} = 7$$

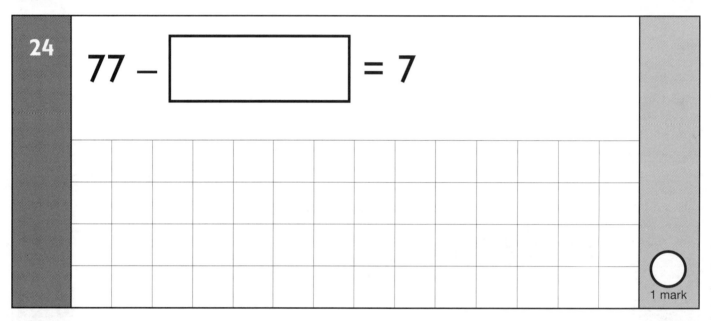

1 mark

25

$$\frac{1}{4} \text{ of } 20 = \boxed{}$$

1 mark

End of test

Key Stage 1

Set A

Mathematics

Paper 2: reasoning

An adult will read the instructions to you for the first five questions. You will answer the remaining questions on your own.

First Name	
Last Name	

Characters and Names

James and Anisa are children who are in some of the questions. There are different children mentioned in other questions as well. Their names are Eve, Sanjay, Fatima and Max.

James　　　　**Anisa**

Eve　　　　Sanjay　　　　Fatima　　　　Max

Practice question

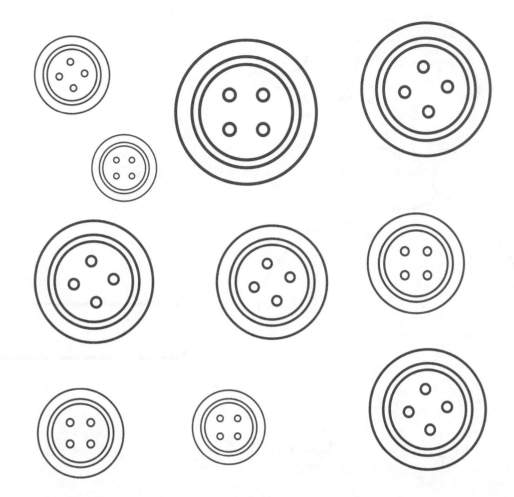

1

	p

2

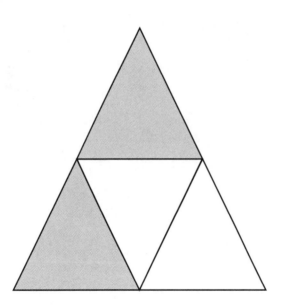

$\frac{3}{4}$ ☐ $\frac{1}{2}$ ☐

$\frac{1}{3}$ ☐ $\frac{1}{4}$ ☐

3

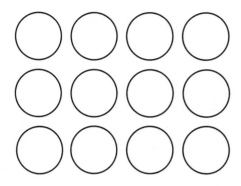

3 + 4 ☐   4 + 4 ☐

3 × 4 ☐   3 − 4 ☐

4

| 15 | 105 | 150 | 115 | 155 |

5

| 15 | | 25 |

Now continue with the rest of the paper on your own.

6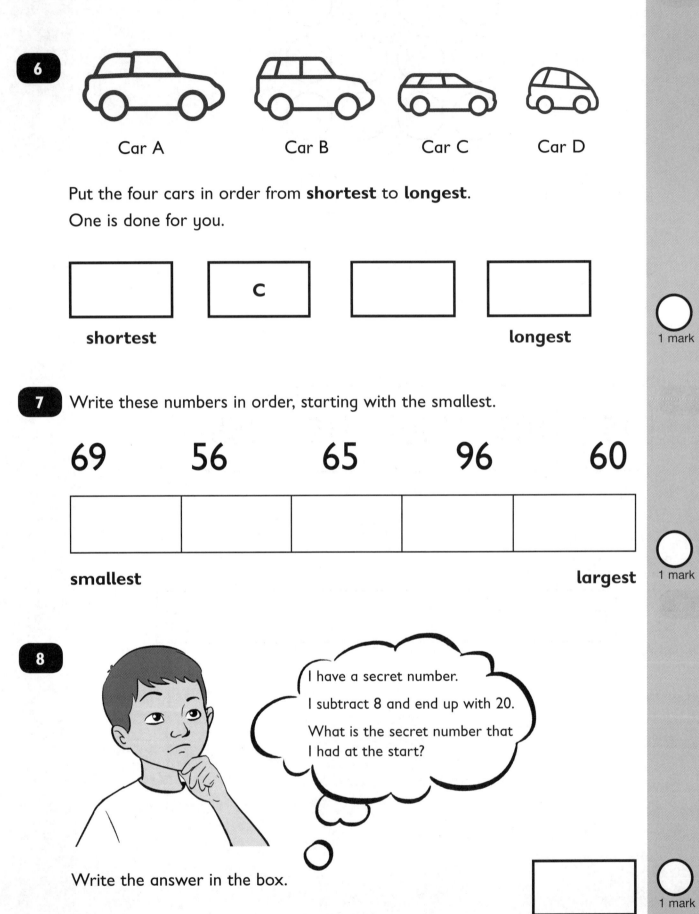

Car A   Car B   Car C   Car D

Put the four cars in order from **shortest** to **longest**.
One is done for you.

	C		
shortest			**longest**

○ 1 mark

7 Write these numbers in order, starting with the smallest.

69   56   65   96   60

smallest   **largest**

○ 1 mark

8

I have a secret number.

I subtract 8 and end up with 20.

What is the secret number that I had at the start?

Write the answer in the box.

○ 1 mark

9 Put a tick next to the **third black section** on the counting stick.

first

1 mark

10 Circle the **two** numbers that are odd.

15   56   39   90

1 mark

11 Anisa has **50** sweets in a jar.

She gives **15** to Sanjay.

How many sweets does Anisa have **left**?

| sweets |

1 mark

12 Fatima's sunflower was **60cm** tall.

It grows **9cm** taller.

How tall is the sunflower now?

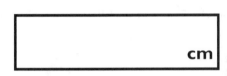 cm 1 mark

13 Measure the longest side.

Use a ruler.

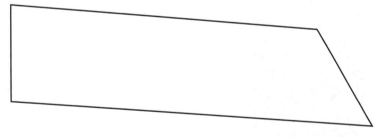

 cm 1 mark

14 This pictogram shows the vehicles passing James's house in 1 hour.

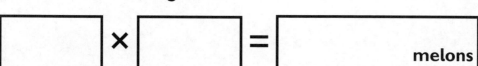

key:

 = 1 car

= 1 bicycle

= 1 van

= 1 lorry

= 1 bus

a) How many bicycles passed James's house?

| bicycles |

b) More cars passed James's house than buses.

How many **more**?

| cars |

15 A shop has **8** crates to hold melons.

Each crate holds **5** melons.

Complete the number sentence to show how many melons there are **altogether**.

| | × | | = | melons |

16 Fill in the missing numbers to make each pair of cards **total 20**.

One pair is done for you.

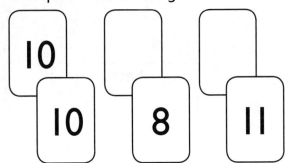

1 mark

17 Here are three numbers.

 17 27 44

Use these numbers to create four number sentences.

 + 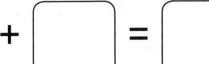 =

 + 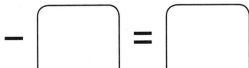 =

 −  =

 − =
1 mark

18 Anisa has **50p** in 5p coins.

How many 5p coins does Anisa have?

 **coins**

1 mark

19 Write six **different** numbers to make these sums correct.

☐ + ☐ = **35**

☐ + ☐ = **35**

☐ + ☐ = **35**

2 marks

20 Tick **three** shapes that **do not** contain a **right angle**.

1 mark

21 One train passes through a station every hour.

How many trains pass through the station in **1 day**?

	trains

1 mark

22 James, Eve, Max and Fatima have 4 marbles each.

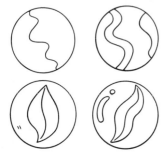

How many marbles do they have **altogether**?

	marbles

1 mark

23 Here is part of a number line.

Write the correct number in the box.

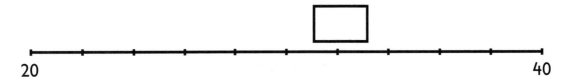

20   40

1 mark

24 Sanjay buys **2** packets of crisps and **3** chocolate bars.

25p

10p

How much does he spend **altogether**?

Show your working

p

2 marks

25 Tick the shape that has exactly $\frac{1}{3}$ shaded.

1 mark

26 Eve is facing South (S).

She turns clockwise and is now facing North (N).

Compete the sentence to describe the turn that Eve made.

Eve turned clockwise through [   ] right angles.

1 mark

27 Look at the measuring jugs.

A

B

The amount of water is lower in jug A than jug B.
How much lower?

[   ] ml

1 mark

28 Fatima has **6** bags of tomatoes.

Write a number sentence using **x** and **=** to show that Fatima has **30** tomatoes altogether.

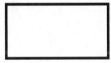

1 mark

29 Write the symbols **x** (multiply), **÷** (divide) or **=** (equals) to make the number sentence below correct.

60 ☐ 5 ☐ 12

1 mark

30 James has **8** bunches of grapes.

Each bunch has **10** grapes.

James gives **30** grapes to his friends.

How many grapes does he have left?

Show your working

| grapes |

2 marks

31 The sugar weighs **55** grams.

The sugar and the flour together weigh **98** grams.

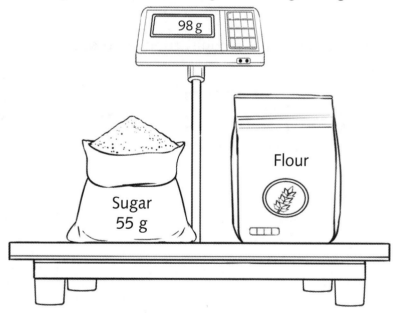

What does the flour weigh?

| grams |

1 mark

End of test

Key Stage 1

Set B

Mathematics

Paper 1: arithmetic

First Name	
Last Name	

Practice question

$$7 + 1 = \boxed{}$$

1

$8 - 5 = $ ⬚

1 mark

2

$5 + 9 = $ ⬚

1 mark

3

$41 + 8 = $ ⬚

1 mark

4

$10 + 10 + 10 =$ ⬚

1 mark

5

$79 - 9 =$ ⬚

1 mark

6

$7 \times 10 =$ ⬚

1 mark

7

$80 - 70 = \boxed{}$

1 mark

8

$\dfrac{1}{2}$ of $10 = \boxed{}$

1 mark

9

$\boxed{} - 10 = 16$

1 mark

10

$$67 + 11 = \boxed{}$$

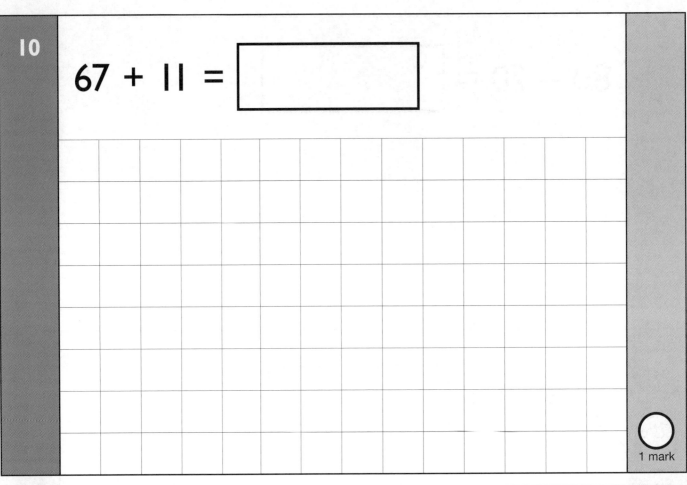

1 mark

11

$$12 \div 3 = \boxed{}$$

1 mark

12

9 + 78 = [ ]

13

41 + 54 = [ ]

14

$10 \times 2 = \boxed{}$

○ 1 mark

15

$30 + \boxed{} = 80$

○ 1 mark

16

$99 - 8 = \boxed{}$

○ 1 mark

17

$7 \times 0 =$ ⬚

18

$56 - 32 =$ ⬚

19

$$29 + 71 = \boxed{}$$

20

$$72 - 35 = \boxed{}$$

21

$$45 \div 5 = \boxed{}$$

22

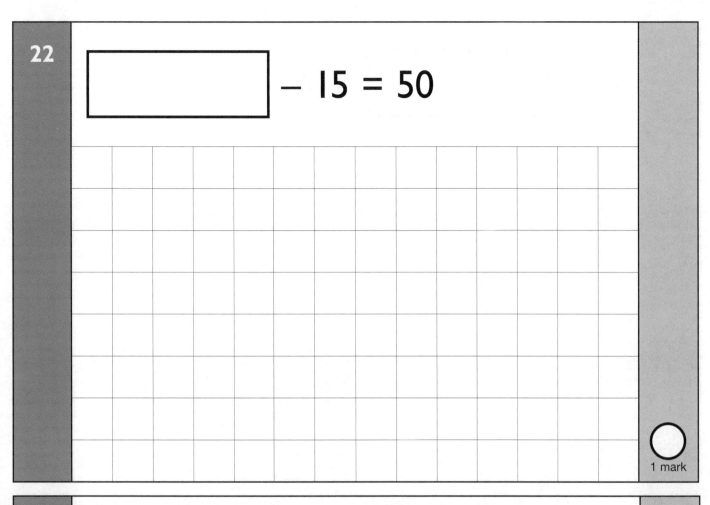

$$\boxed{} - 15 = 50$$

1 mark

23

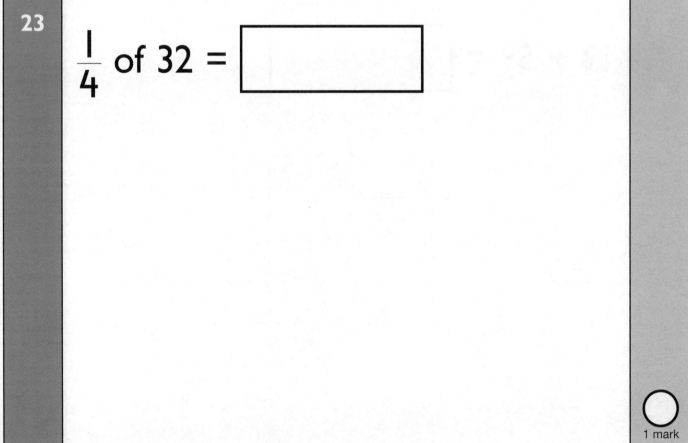

$$\frac{1}{4} \text{ of } 32 = \boxed{}$$

1 mark

24

$$17 - \boxed{} = 7$$

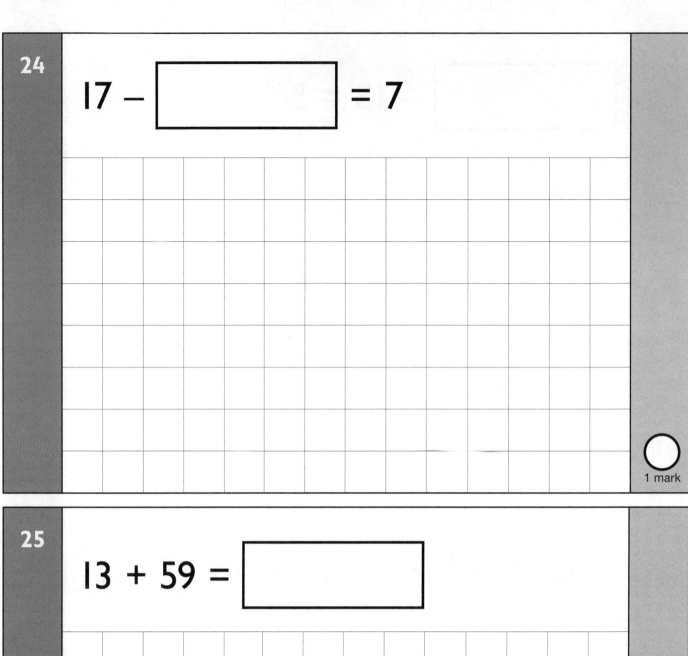

1 mark

25

$$13 + 59 = \boxed{}$$

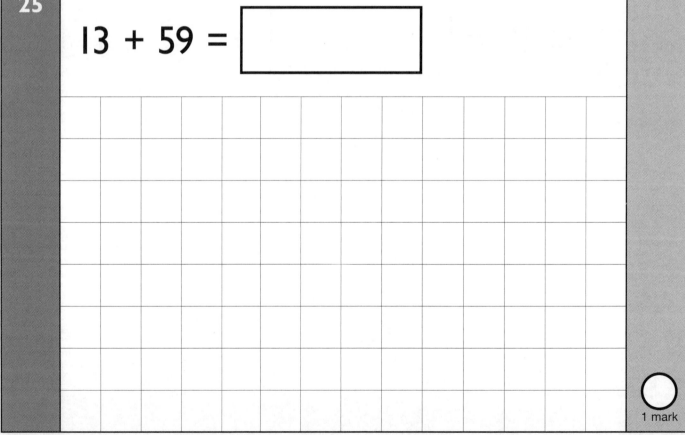

1 mark

End of test

Key Stage 1

Set B

Mathematics

Paper 2: reasoning

An adult will read the instructions to you for the first five questions. You will answer the remaining questions on your own.

First Name	
Last Name	

Characters and Names

James and Anisa are children who are in some of the questions. There are different children mentioned in other questions as well. Their names are Eve, Sanjay, Fatima and Max.

James   **Anisa**

Eve   Sanjay   Fatima   Max

Practice question

marbles

1 93   92   91   90 ☐ ☐

2 $30 - 5 - 5 =$ ☐

3

☐ **buttons**

4  × ☐ = 100

5

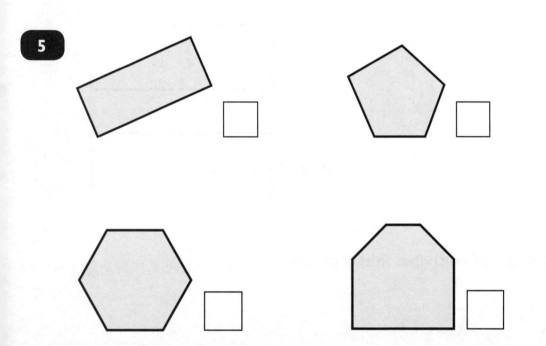

Now continue with the rest of the paper on your own.

6 Use **all** of the digits below to write the **smallest** and **largest** number possible.

| 6 | 1 | 9 |

Smallest [   ]

Largest [   ]

1 mark

7 Tick the names of the three shapes in this picture.

Tick **three**.

triangle ☐

square ☐

rectangle ☐

circle ☐

hexagon ☐

1 mark

8 Circle the **longest** time.

65 minutes   1 hour   15 minutes   45 minutes

1 mark

9 Look at the sequence.

◯ ☆ ▢ △ ◯ ☆ ▢ △ ◯ . . .

Tick the next shape in the sequence.

◯   ☆   ▢   △

10 James has **9** pencil cases. He puts **5** pencils in each pencil case.

How many pencils are in the pencil cases **altogether**?

pencils

11

25p

Eve buys **one** biscuit for 25p.

She pays with a 50p coin.

How much change does she get?

p

12 There are **10** satsumas in each net bag and **7** more loose satsumas.

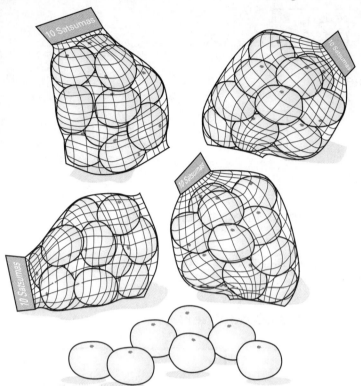

How many satsumas are there **altogether**?

	satsumas

13 Anisa makes **32** using different shapes for tens and ones.

She then makes a new number.

What is Anisa's new number?

14 Look at these numbers.

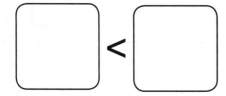

Write each number **once** to make these correct.

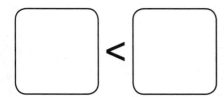

15 Here is a number sentence:

25 + 27 = 52

Use this number sentence to help you fill in the missing numbers below.

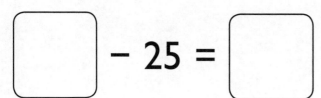

○ 1 mark

16

 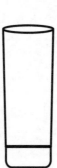 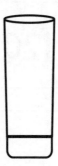 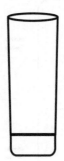

○ 1 mark

Sanjay has 30 ice cubes and 5 glasses.

He puts the same number of ice cubes in each glass.

How many ice cubes go in each glass?

ice cubes

○ 1 mark

17 Look at these coins:

What is the largest amount of money you can make using **four** of these coins?

 p

1 mark

18 Here is part of a number line.

Write the correct numbers in the boxes.

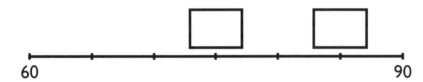

60   90

1 mark

19 Use only these numbers to make a **different** number sentence each time.

| 120 | 10 | 12 |

One is done for you.

10 × 12 = 120

☐ × ☐ = ☐

☐ ÷ ☐ = ☐

1 mark

20 Anisa and Max count buses.

Anisa counts **47** red buses.

Max counts **45** yellow buses.

How many do they count **altogether**?

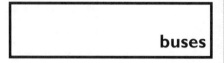
buses

1 mark

21 One length of a running track is **10** metres.

Fatima runs the length of the track **4** times.

Fatima works out how many metres she runs altogether.

Circle the **two** calculations that she can use.

10 + 4

4 x 10

10 + 10 + 10 + 10

4 + 4 + 4 + 4

1 mark

22 Use four different number cards to complete the number sentences below.

| 10 | 30 | 70 | 35 | 50 | 45 |

$$\boxed{} + \boxed{} = 80$$

$$\boxed{} + \boxed{} = 80$$

◯ 2 marks

23 Tick the two **cuboids**.

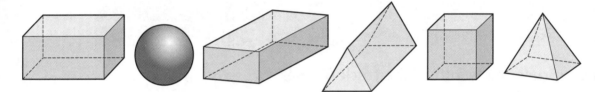

◯ 1 mark

24 How much water is in the measuring jug?

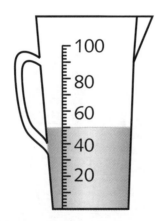

100
80
60
40
20

ml

◯ 1 mark

25 20 children choose their favourite animal.

The chart shows the results.

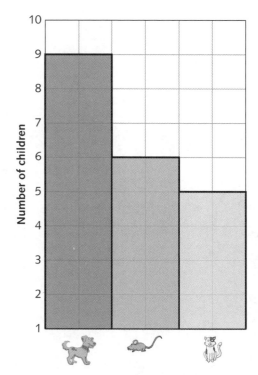

a) How many more children choose dog than mouse?

	children

b) Another girl joins the group. She chooses cat.

Add this information to the chart.

26 Complete these number sentences.

One is done for you.

$4 + 6 = 10$

$44 + \boxed{} = 50$

$\boxed{} + 6 = 100$

27 Look at these four toys.

Fatima buys **three different** toys.

She spends exactly **£1**

Tick the **three** toys that Fatima buys.

1 mark

28 Write the **same** number in both boxes to make the sum correct.

☐ + ☐ = 30

1 mark

29 There are **75** cakes.

25 boys and **30** girls each take a cake.

How many cakes are **left**?

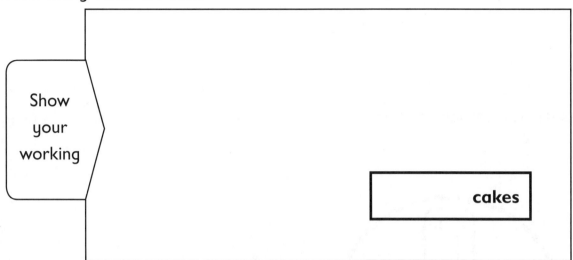

Show your working

| | cakes |

2 marks

30 Tick the shape that has $\frac{1}{3}$ shaded.

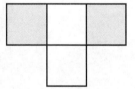

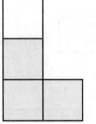

1 mark

31 Write the missing number in the box.

$$16 - 6 = 10 +\ \boxed{}$$

32 This dial is currently pointing at **0**.

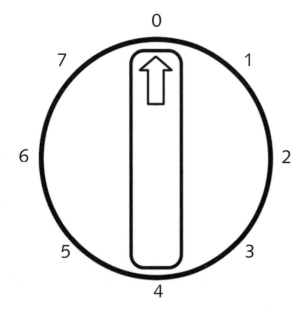

Complete the sentence to describe the turn needed for the dial to be pointing at **6**.

Turn the dial through $\boxed{}$ right angle(s) clockwise.

End of test

Key Stage 1

Set C

Mathematics

Paper 1: arithmetic

First Name	
Last Name	

Practice question

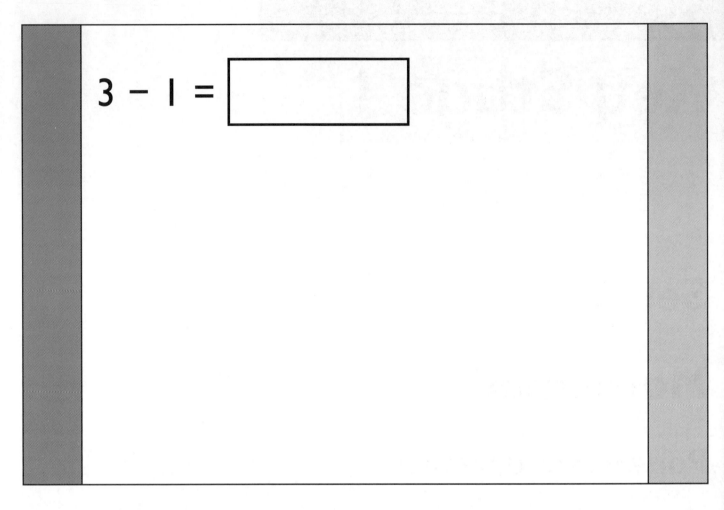

3 − 1 = ☐

1

4 + 6 = ⬚

2

9 – 9 = ⬚

3

50 + 50 = ⬚

4

$\dfrac{1}{2}$ of 12 =

◯
1 mark

5

100 − 1 =

◯
1 mark

6

120 − 10 =

◯
1 mark

7   90 ÷ 10 = [ ]

1 mark

8   20 + 50 = [ ]

1 mark

9   8 × 10 = [ ]

1 mark

10 88 + 9 = [ ]

1 mark

11 6 + 3 + 5 = [ ]

1 mark

12 9 × 2 = [ ]

1 mark

13

$5 + 93 =$ ⬚

1 mark

14

$\frac{1}{2}$ of $24 =$ ⬚

1 mark

15

$30 +$ ⬚ $= 80$

1 mark

16

$$78 - 14 = \boxed{}$$

17

$$38 + 59 = \boxed{}$$

18

$5 \times 11 =$ ☐

1 mark

19

$72 - 40 =$ ☐

1 mark

20

$5 +$ ⬜ $+ 5 = 25$

21

$61 - 36 =$ ⬜

22

$18 \div 2 = $

23

$\dfrac{1}{3}$ of $18 = $

24

$$\boxed{} - 20 = 48$$

25

$$38 + 45 = \boxed{}$$

End of test

Key Stage 1

Set C

Mathematics

Paper 2: reasoning

An adult will read the instructions to you for the first five questions. You will answer the remaining questions on your own.

First Name	
Last Name	

Characters and Names

James and Anisa are children who are in some of the questions. There are different children mentioned in other questions as well. Their names are Eve, Sanjay, Fatima and Max.

James   **Anisa**

Eve   Sanjay   Fatima   Max

Practice question

1

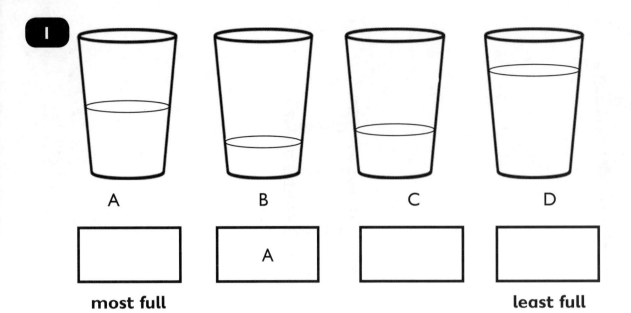

	A		
most full			**least full**

1 mark

2

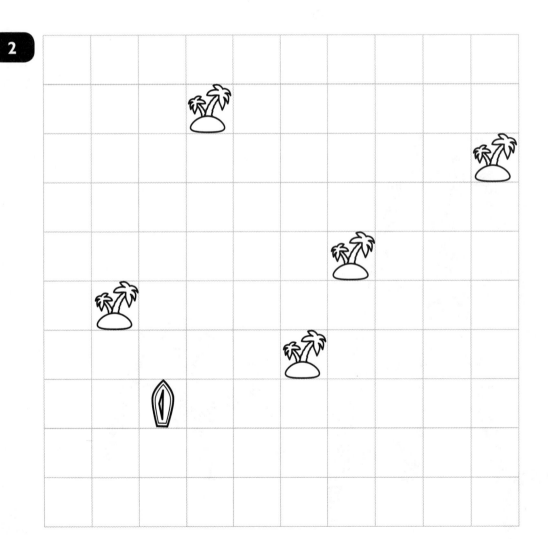

1 mark

3

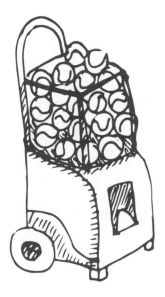

tennis balls

1 mark

4

p

1 mark

5

 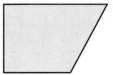

  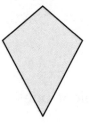

1 mark

Now continue with the rest of the paper on your own.

6 Look at the sequence.

0 ☐ 6 9 ☐

Write the missing numbers in the boxes.

○ 1 mark

7

It has six tens and eight ones.

Write the answer in the box.

○ 1 mark

8 Shade $\frac{2}{4}$ of this shape.

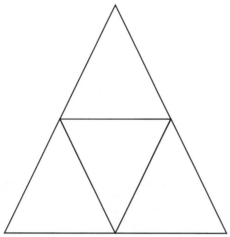

9 A coat costs £32.

Eve has £25.

How much **more** money does she need to buy the coat?

£ [ ]

10 A purse has these 8 coins inside.

What fraction of the coins are 10p coins?

Circle the correct fraction.

$\dfrac{1}{3}$ $\dfrac{1}{2}$ $\dfrac{1}{4}$ $\dfrac{2}{4}$

1 mark

11 Anisa goes on four bus journeys each week.

Which journey lasts the **longest?**

Tick the journey that lasts the longest.

Journey to School	Journey to Swimming	Journey to the Seaside	Journey to Drama Club
35 minutes	half an hour	65 minutes	2 hours

1 mark

12 Look at the clock.

What time does the clock show?

Tick the correct box.

1 o'clock	half past 1
quarter to 1	quarter past 1

1 mark

13 Sanjay saves £5 per week.

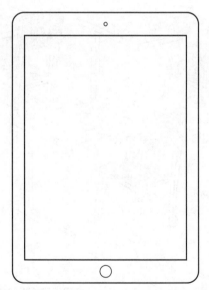

He wants to buy a tablet computer. It costs £60.

How many weeks will he have to save up for?

weeks

1 mark

14 The pictogram shows the number of buttons four children have.

James	⊙ ⊙ ⊙ ⊙ ⊙ ⊙
Anisa	⊙ ⊙ ⊙
Sanjay	⊙ ⊙ ⊙ ⊙ ⊙ ⊙ ⊙ ⊙ ⊙ ⊙
Max	⊙ ⊙ ⊙ ⊙ ⊙ ⊙ ⊙ ⊙

Sanjay has more buttons than Anisa.

How many **more**?

	buttons

1 mark

15 **50** new pencils are shared equally among **5** tables in a classroom.

How many pencils does **each** table get?

	pencils

1 mark

16 A school raises money for charity.

Class 1 collects **£32**.

Class 2 collects **£49**.

How much money did they collect **altogether**?

£ _____

17 Tick the shapes that do **not** have a line of symmetry.

18 Eve ate half an apple.

Which fraction shows the amount she ate?

Circle it.

$\frac{1}{3}$ $\frac{1}{4}$ $\frac{2}{4}$ $\frac{2}{3}$

1 mark

19 All the children in Year 2 are put into **10** teams for sports day.

There are **2** boys and **2** girls in each team.

How many children are in Year 2 **altogether**?

| children |

1 mark

20 There are **62** people in a cafe.

19 more people go into the cafe.

Then **45** people go out.

How many people are in the cafe **now**?

Show your working

| people |

2 marks

21 The numbers on this number line go up by the **same amount** each time.

Write the missing numbers in the boxes.

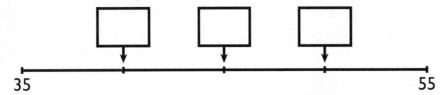

35   55

1 mark

22 **27 strawberries** are shared between a group of friends at a party.

They each get **3 strawberries**.

How many friends were there?

 **friends**

1 mark

23 James has **80p**.

James has **25p** more than Anisa.

Tick the coins that Anisa has.

1 mark

24 Write the missing number to make this number sentence correct.

$$12 - 8 = \boxed{} + 2$$

1 mark

25 Sanjay rolls three dice and adds the scores together.

He rolls a fourth dice. His total score is now **21**.

What was the score on the **fourth dice**?

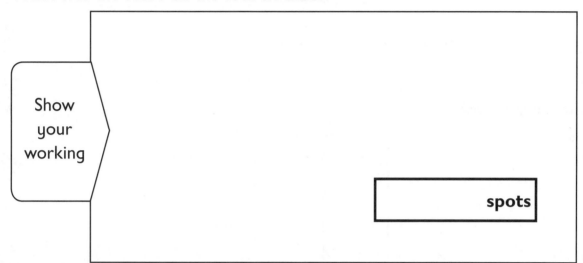

Show your working

spots

2 marks

26 Fatima makes a pattern with sticks.

Some sticks are long and some are short.

Fatima writes a number pattern on the sticks.

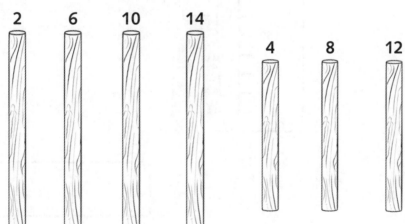

Write the number that will be on the next **long** stick.

1 mark

27 Draw dotted lines to divide this square into quarters.

Use the dots to help you.

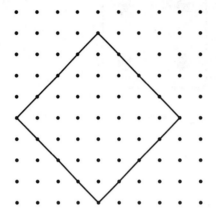

28 How tall is James?

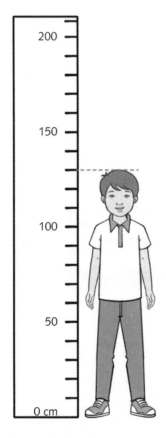

	cm

29 Draw a rectangle **8cm** long and **4cm** wide.

Use a ruler.

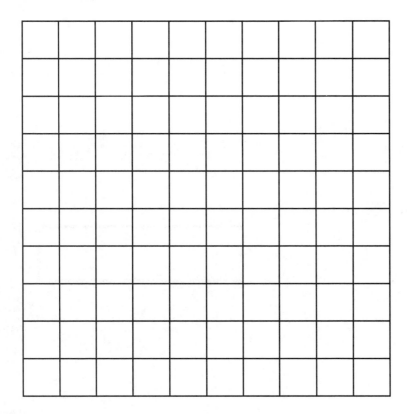

30 **Three** of these shapes have **more than 4** vertices.

Tick them.

 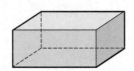 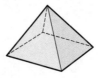

31 Write two numbers that are greater than 30 and less than 40 to make this subtraction correct.

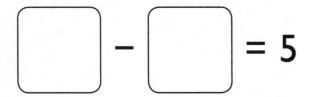

$$\boxed{} - \boxed{} = 5$$

32 Look at the grid below.

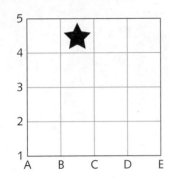

a) Which square is the star 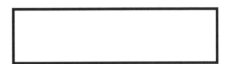 in?

1 mark

b) Draw an X in square D3.

1 mark

End of test